fiber&cord
jewelry

Easy to Make Projects
Using Paracord, Hemp,
Leather, and More

KB
KALMBACH BOOKS

Ashley K. Bunting

Kalmbach Books
21027 Crossroads Circle
Waukesha, Wisconsin 53186
www.Kalmbach.com/Books

Published in 2015
19 18 17 16 15   1 2 3 4 5

Manufactured in the United States of America
ISBN: 978-1-62700-121-2
EISBN: 978-1-62700-127-4

Editor: Karin Van Voorhees
Book Design: Lisa Schroeder
Photographer: Jim Forbes

Library of Congress Control Number: 2014950470

contents

introduction

Material is my inspiration. I love picking up an item and really dissecting it. What are its elements? How can it be altered? What are its characteristics? What does it represent? Does it have cultural significance? For years I worked for a bead shop as their head designer. I would be given a new bead, bauble, or supply and I'd go to work. It was my job to translate this material into an inspiring piece of jewelry.

The genesis of this book was the sudden popularity of parachute cord (paracord). It was everywhere, and I had no interest in the macraméd survival bracelets sweeping the nation's craft stores. I set myself on the task of using paracord—this new, easily obtainable material—in a way that excited me. Rather than using a masculine cord in a utilitarian way, I used it to contrast feminine design elements.

My research expanded to other fibers and cords. I discovered new applications for materials I previously had no interest in. It was rewarding to realize that these materials could be formed and sculpted. Instead of just using cord as a stringing material, I could use it to alter other components. I kept asking myself, How can I take a common, well-known material and use it in new, exciting, and unique ways?

For me, this is the creative process. I am most passionate when I use design as a way of solving a problem.

In this book you will discover new techniques for common cords and fibers. I encourage you to look at hemp, jute, leather, paracord, lace, and ribbon in a new light and see the awesome potential these materials hold. By exploring and identifying the unique characteristics of each of these materials, you can discover untapped design opportunities.

Use this book as a stepping stone. My hope is that you will try my projects and experiment with my techniques, and that doing so will encourage you to approach materials you've never used before, or previously not been interested in, and examine them with new interest. Cut, twist, knot, melt, stack, and wrap your way to discovering a love of fibers and cords.

AKBUNTING

materials

paracord

Paracord is made of synthetic nylon fibers. It's a kernmantle rope, meaning it has a core, or "kern", and it has an outer sheath or "mantle." It comes in fabulous neon colors. Paracord can be easily frayed or even melted. It was originally used as safety cord; therefore it is very strong. Paracord is inexpensive, easy to find, and comes in a few different sizes. The projects in this book use paracord 550; most craft stores carry it.

hemp

Hemp is a natural fiber made from the cannabis plant. Hemp comes in a huge array of thicknesses, either in its natural color or dyed. Some hemp has a rougher texture; I like working with softer carded hemp. Hemp can be purchased in small bundles or large skeins.

jute

Jute is a vegetable fiber made from the jute plant. Jute is the fiber used to make burlap, and it's wonderfully fuzzy as a cord. It can be natural in color or dyed, and is usually relatively thin but can be found in thicker sizes. Find jute in colorful variety packs at craft stores; lower-quality jute can be found at garden shops.

cotton

Cotton cord often comes waxed. The waxed cord is great for making very durable, water-resistant jewelry. For the projects in this book I prefer unwaxed cotton. Most cotton cord is about 1–2mm in diameter and comes in all kinds of colors. You can often find it by the yard at your local bead shop or in multipacks at craft stores.

waxed linen

I really like waxed linen. It is nice and thin (it can go through most beads) and it's super strong. I use waxed linen mostly in a supporting role, to string a project or connect components. It comes in a ton of colors. The only downfall is it usually is only sold on big spools that can be pricey.

trim

I recently discovered trim packs in the girls hair accessory section in craft stores. These happy bundles offer a great way to get a little selection of a bunch of styles. If you sew, save all your bits of leftovers for jewelry projects.

leather

Leather is soft, flexible, and strong. Leather is affected by heat. It is recyclable. I love to thrift shop, and thrift stores are a great place to get leather. Buy old leather jackets, pants, and skirts, disassemble the pieces, and you've got a ton of gorgeous leather at a fraction of the price of retail.

ribbon

There seem to be a billion kinds of ribbon: brocade, silk, glitter, sheer, wired, etc. In my area we have a few odd-lot stores. I love searching these shops for ribbon, lace, and trim. You can find unique spools of super-cheap ribbons. You also can shop for ribbon at craft stores or fabric stores.

leather cord and lacing

Leather cord comes in many colors, sizes, and finishes. You can usually find it by the foot at your local bead store or by the spool at craft stores. Leather lacing is a long strip of leather originally used to sew leather pieces together. It comes in a wide variety of colors, widths, and thicknesses. Look for high-quality deer hide lacing, too.

lace

When you buy lace, make sure that it's made of cotton. It looks much nicer, it has better movement and stretch, and wears nicely over time. If you're having trouble finding a color you like, it's easy to dye cotton lace.

tools

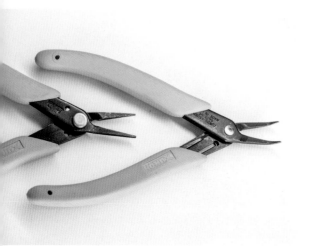

bentnose and chainnose pliers

You'll use these two pliers in almost every project. Bentnose and chainnose pliers are used for any sort of bending, folding, or holding of wire. They are also used for opening and closing jump rings and work as an extension of your hand. The chainnose pliers pictured (that I like the most) are actually called "tweezer nose" pliers. They are very fine, precise, and great for getting into small areas, but they are still very strong. The bentnose version of the tweezer nose is incredibly handy. The bend allows your arm and wrist to stay in a more natural position. The bend also gives you a better grip when opening jump rings and holding onto wrapped loops.

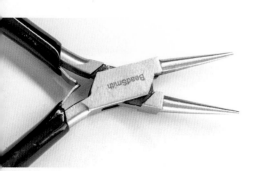

roundnose

Roundnose pliers are used for creating loops. Use them more like a mandrel to shape wire, than as a gripping or bending tool. Make sure the tips taper from very small to a larger diameter. This will give you the most versatility when making different sized loops.

wire snips

Wire snips are used for cutting any soft wires (like copper or craft wire) up to 18 gauge. Never cut steel wire with your good wire snips. The finer the tip of your snips, the closer you will be able to trim your wires. The wire snips pictured here are a great basic flush-cutting snip.

hard wire snips

Hard wire snips are designed to cut heavy steel wire such as memory wire.

metal hole punch

The metal hole punch is a great tool. Not only can you add holes to metal components with it, but this hole punch is also great for piercing leather. I like to use tools that cross over and can be multifunctional.

awl

An awl is basically a pointy metal stick. Awls are often used in pearl knotting to guide the knots, however they are very useful for other jewelry-making tasks. In this book I use an awl for poking holes in leather. It is also good for applying glues, moving around components that are being glued, or for poking holes in earring cards for craft fairs.

high-durability scissors

Heavy duty! These scissors are the real deal—they will cut anything (including the top off your Christmas tree, which I do not recommend). They are perfect for cutting heavy leather cording and stacks of leather. One of the blades is serrated, which helps catch slippery cords in its jaw. Paracord can be cut nice and cleanly with high-durability scissors.

fabric scissors

Always have a nice, sharp pair of fabric scissors on hand. These scissors are best when cutting sheets of material like recycled leather. Try not to cut any metal scraps or sticky materials with your fabric scissors.

big eye needle

The Big Eye needle is by far my favorite needle. There is no traditional eye. The whole needle has a slit, and when you open the slit, you can thread the needle with almost any thickness of cord or material. It is a good idea to have a few Big Eye needles on hand because they can bend out of shape and break over time.

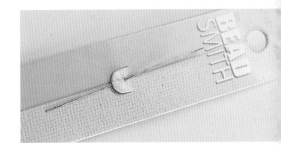

butane lighter

A good flame fuses the cut ends of paracord and keeps the cord from unraveling. I prefer a refillable butane lighter. The flame is much hotter and more precise than a disposable lighter. I also find them easier to hold and more economical since they can be refilled. You can purchase butane cartridges from a local hardware store.

cord scissors

These little scissors are one of my favorite new tools. They are ridiculously sharp and the blades are small, which allows you to cut super close to your work. Another huge advantage to these scissors is that they eliminate the traditional finger loops that just tend to get in the way when making quick, simple cord cuts.

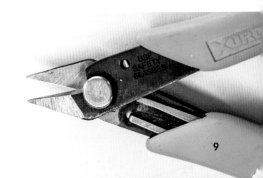

glues

Krazy glue gel

Most everyone has used a cyanoacrylate glue like Krazy or superglue. The gel version is great for jewelry and crafts. It is thicker which keeps the glue right where you put it.

E6000 jewelry adhesive

This is my go-to glue. It is an epoxy, meaning it dries in a rubbery, flexible state as opposed to a smooth, hard state like cyanoacrylates. E6000 jewelry adhesive is best when gluing nonporous materials like glass, stone, or metal. It holds remarkably well.

white school glue

When diluted 50/50 with water, plain old white glue acts as a good stiffener for lace.

superglue pen

When I first bought a pen like this I didn't think the dabber tip would do the trick. However, it has proven to be very helpful. The tip has to be depressed to release glue, which helps control the amount you dispense. Use this pen when you only want a tiny bit of glue.

techniques

opening and closing a jump ring

1 Use two pairs of chainnose pliers, or a pair of chainnose pliers and a pair of bentnose pliers. Hold one pair of pliers in each hand. Flatly grasp one side of the jump ring in each plier, with the ring's opening between the pliers.

2 Push the pliers in opposite directions to swing the ring open, like opening a door. To close the ring, repeat this action in the opposite direction. Opening a ring in this way preserves the perfectly round shape of the ring.

making a simple loop

1 String a bead onto a headpin **(a)**.

2 Right where the headpin meets the bead, bend the headpin just shy of a 90-degree angle **(b)**.

3 Using roundnose pliers grasp the headpin next to the bend **(c)**.

4 Use your finger to bend the wire up and over the pliers until it hits the far side of the bead **(d)**.

5 The loop is starting to form around the top jaw of the pliers. Reposition the pliers so the bottom jaw is inside the loop that is beginning to form.

6 Pull the headpin under the roundnose pliers to complete the bottom of the loop **(e)**.

7 Trim the remaining wire so the wire of the loop does not overlap **(f)**.

8 The finished loop **(g)**.

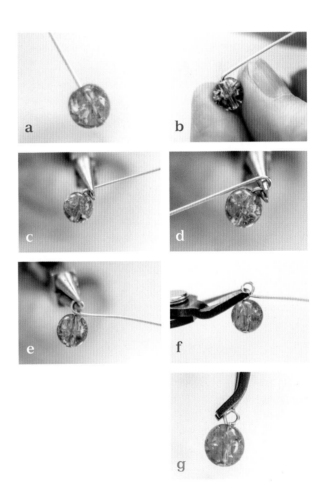

a

b

c

d

e

f

g

making a wrapped loop

1 String a bead onto a headpin **(a)**.

2 Using chainnose pliers, grasp the headpin directly above the bead. Bend the headpin over the pliers at a 90-degree angle **(b)**.

3 Using roundnose pliers, grasp the headpin next to the bend **(c)**.

4 Use your finger to bend the wire up and over the pliers **(d)**.

5 The loop is starting to form around the top jaw of the pliers. Reposition the pliers so the bottom jaw is inside the loop that is beginning to form. Pull the headpin under the roundnose pliers to complete the bottom of the loop **(e)**.

9 Remove the roundnose pliers and grasp the loop with chainnose pliers. Wrap the tail of the headpin around the wire under the loop **(f)**.

10 Fill the space between the loop and the bead with wrapping. Trim any remaining wire tail **(g)**.

11 The finished loop **(h)**.

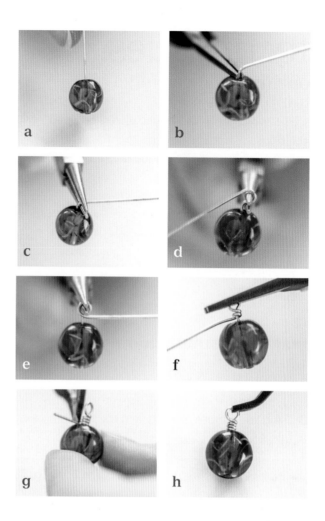

making a double loop

1 String components onto a headpin **(a)**.

2 Trim the headpin. Use your finger width as a length guide **(b)**.

3 Grasp the end of the headpin with roundnose pliers, and begin to roll down **(c)**.

4 Adjust and reposition the pliers so you can continue to roll down towards the components. Roll down until two loops form and all the components are snugly held together **(d)**.

5 Front view **(e)**. Back view **(f)**.

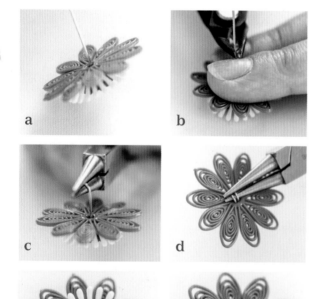

paracord

tubes

links

flowers

bead

melt

tassels

fray

beachcomber's
wrap-around bracelet

This beginner project is a good way to become familiar with making paracord tubes. Paracord tubes open a brand new way of using paracord—you'll make your very own beads from the cord. The accent beads used in this project are just suggestions. Collect leftovers, bits, and baubles and design your own Beach Comber Bracelet.

MATERIALS
- 14mm gray agate round with channel-set rhinestones
- **2** 12mm silver starfish buttons
- 11mm milk glass irregular round
- **4** 10mm crystal rounds
- 10mm matte gray glass round
- **4** 10mm matte crystal rondelles
- **3** 8mm crystal rounds
- **2** 8mm silver African rounds
- **2** 5mm crystal rounds
- 21 in. navy paracord 550
- 21 in. gray paracord 550
- 21 in. medium blue paracord 550
- 8½ coils flat silver-plated memory wire

TOOLS
- high-durability scissors
- chainnose pliers
- roundnose pliers
- steel wire cutters
- butane lighter

a

1 Cut seven pieces of each paracord color in a variety of lengths ranging from 1½–3 in.

2 Remove the inner white core, or kern, from all pieces of paracord **(a)**.

⑥ tip
Flat memory wire holds its shape better than many of the other memory wires on the market today. It also has an attractive finished look when the ends are turned in, forming cute spirals.

3 Using the butane lighter, carefully melt the ends of all the paracord pieces to prevent fraying **(b)**.

4 Using steel wire cutters (absolutely do not use your good wire snips), cut the memory wire to a length of 8½ coils. With roundnose pliers, make a loop at one end of the memory wire **(c)**.

5 String the paracord tubes and beads on the memory wire: String one gray tube, a bead, one black tube, a bead or button, one blue tube, and a bead or button **(d)**.

6 Repeat until there is only about ¾ in. of memory wire uncovered. Make a loop at the other end of the wire.

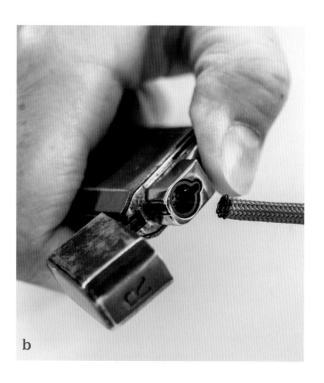

b

c

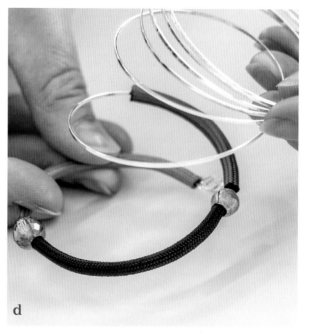

d

swing & sway earrings

Colorful, playful, and a lot of fun—these earrings are super easy to make in any color combo. This is another good project for practicing making paracord tubes. Master this simple technique and use it to design your own custom paracord pieces.

MATERIALS
- 20 in. 1mm silver-plated cable chain
- 5 in. hot pink paracord 550
- 8 in. lime paracord 550
- pair of silver-plated earring wires

TOOLS
- high-durability scissors
- wire snips
- chainnose pliers
- butane lighter

⊙ tip
Having trouble getting your chains the exact same length? Cut your pieces of chain and slide the end link of each chain piece onto a piece of wire. Let the chains hang. This way, you can easily see any difference in length and trim accordingly.

1 Cut two 4-in. pieces of chain and two 6-in. pieces of chain. Cut two 2½-in. pieces of pink paracord and two 4-in. pieces of green paracord.

2 Remove the inner white core, or kern, of all pieces of paracord. Use the butane lighter to slightly melt each end of the paracord pieces to prevent fraying.

3 String a 4-in. piece of chain through a pink paracord tube and a 6-in. piece of chain through a green paracord tube **(a)**.

4 Open an earring wire loop (Techniques) and string an end link of the 6-in. chain onto the loop. String an end link of the 4-in. chain. Repeat with the remaining chain ends in the opposite order **(b)**. Close the earring wire loop.

5 Make a second earring.

a

b

itty bitty tassel necklace

Like tiny bursts of color, tassels are adorable and add color and movement to jewelry. Because paracord is easy to fray, the tassel-making process is simplified. The number of strings that need to be cut and bound together is greatly reduced. Make a few extra for earrings, or hang one next to the clasp of a bracelet for a fun little charm.

MATERIALS
- 54 in. 3mm curb chain, gunmetal
- 52 in. 20-gauge wire, gunmetal
- 12mm lobster claw clasp, gunmetal
- **9** 6mm jump rings, gunmetal
- 19 in. gray paracord 550
- 9 in. yellow paracord 550
- 9 in. black paracord 550

TOOLS
- high-durability scissors
- chainnose pliers
- roundnose pliers
- wire snips
- awl
- butane lighter

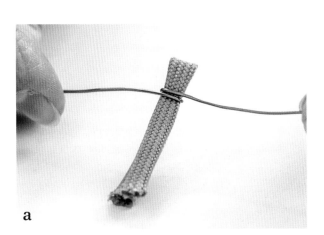

a

b

c

1 Cut three 3-in. pieces of each paracord color and cut two 5-in. pieces of gray paracord. Cut nine 4-in. pieces of wire and two 8-in. pieces of wire. Cut a 16-in., an 18-in., and a 20-in. piece of chain. Remove the inner white core, or kern, from all pieces of paracord.

2 Fold a piece of paracord in half, and wrap a 4-in. piece of wire five times around the paracord to bind **(a)**. Trim the wire tail.

3 Use the awl to fray the paracord **(b)**. Trim the tassel so all the fibers are the same length. Repeat with all paracord pieces.

4 Compare the tassels, and trim so all are the same length **(c)**.

tip
I love pairing flat colors like gray and gun-metal with neon colors. This creates a great contrast and prevents the neon from being too overwhelming.

d

e

f

g

5 Attach the tassels to the chain using jump rings (Techniques) in this manner: 16 in. chain—2 in. from the end add a black tassel, 7 in. from the end add a gray tassel, and 10½ in. from the end add a yellow tassel. 18 in. chain—5 in. from the end add a yellow tassel, 10 in. from the end add a black tassel and 15 in. from the end add a gray tassel. 20 in. chain—4½ in. from the end add a gray tassel, 8 in. from the end add a yellow tassel, and 18½ in. from the end add a black tassel **(d)**.

6 Using the butane lighter, gently melt the ends of the 5-in. pieces of gray paracord to prevent fraying **(e)**.

7 At one end of one 8-in. wire, make a wrapped loop (Techniques). Before completing the wraps, slide on one end of each chain **(f)**. Repeat with the other wire and the other ends of the chains.

h

8 Slide a gray paracord tube over one wire **(g)**, and make a wrapped loop, connecting the lobster claw clasp before completing the wraps. Slide the remaining gray tube over the remaining wire and make a large wrapped loop (large enough for the lobster claw clasp to easily attach) **(h)**.

9 Gently bend the wires in an arch so they are shaped to comfortably fit a neck.

mega fab tassel earrings

The bright paracord colors add to the whimsy of these earrings!

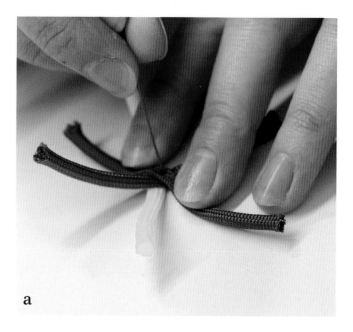

a

MATERIALS
- **2** 10x11mm chevron bead caps, gunmetal
- **2** 2-in. 22-gauge headpins, gunmetal
- pair of earring wires, gunmetal
- 6 in. yellow paracord 550
- 6 in. medium blue paracord 550
- 6 in. blue paracord 550

TOOLS
- high-durability scissors
- chainnose pliers
- bentnose pliers
- roundnose pliers
- wire snips
- awl

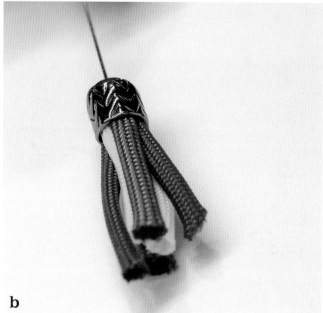

b

1 Cut 3 in. of each paracord color. Remove the inner white core, or kern, from all pieces of paracord.

2 Find the center of each piece of paracord. Use a headpin to pierce through the center of each piece. Splay out the cords so they resemble an asterisk **(a)**.

3 String the headpin up through the cords and the bead cap **(b)**. Make a wrapped loop (Techniques).

c

d

4 Use the awl to fray all the paracord pieces **(c)**.

5 Trim the tassel so all the fibers are the same length.

6 Repeat steps 1–5 to make a second tassel. Compare the two tassels and trim so both are the same length.

7 Attach an earring wire to each tassel **(d)** (Techniques).

urban garden necklace

Paracord is usually neon and flashy, but this project uses a much more subdued color palette. The paracord becomes a textural element and adds depth to the piece. Melting the ends and adhering them together forms these unusual chain links.

1 Cut six 3-in. pieces of dark green paracord. Cut two 5-in. pieces of chain.

2 Place both ends of one piece of paracord into the flame of the butane lighter **(a)**. Quickly press the two melted ends into one another to create an oval link **(b)**. Repeat with all the paracord pieces.

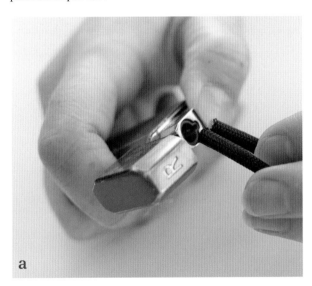

a

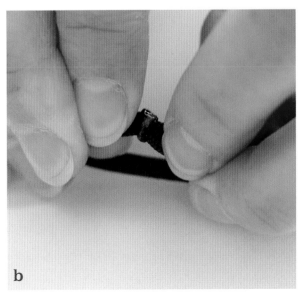

b

MATERIALS

- 31x43mm antiqued brass leaf filigree
- 25mm bronze disk
- 16mm vintage carved mother-of-pearl two-holed button
- **4** 18mm wobbly antiqued brass disks
- **4** 13mm vintage mother-of-pearl two-holed buttons
- 10 in. 6x8mm (open link) antiqued brass cable chain
- **10** 20-gauge gold-plated headpins
- 10mm antique brass round magnetic clasp
- 18 in. dark green paracord 550

TOOLS

- high-durability scissors
- chainnose pliers
- bentnose pliers
- roundnose pliers
- wire snips
- butane lighter

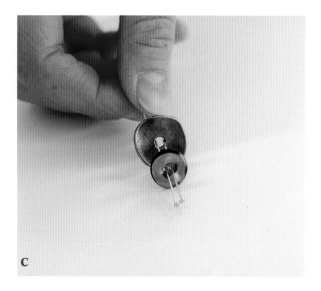

c

d

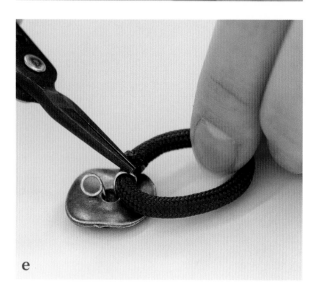

e

3 String a headpin through each hole of one button from front to back and then string both headpins through the hole in a brass disk **(c)**. Make a simple loop large enough to fit around the paracord with each headpin (Techniques) **(d)**. Repeat with the remaining three buttons.

4 Attach two paracord links together by opening the two loops of one button stack and sliding one paracord loop into one headpin loop **(e)**, and another paracord loop into the other headpin loop. Close and tighten the headpin loops. Make sure to hide the seams in the paracord links behind the brass disk.

5 Add another button stack and paracord link to this grouping, so there are three paracord links connected by two button stacks **(f)**. Connect the other three paracord links in the same way.

6 Slide a headpin through each buttonhole of the carved 16mm button. String both headpins through the bronze disks and then through the loop in the filigree leaf **(g)**.

7 With each headpin, turn a simple loop large enough to fit around the paracord **(h)**.

8 Use the simple loops to attach the two sets of connected paracord links together **(i)**: Open a loop, slide in a paracord link, and close the loop.

9 Open the last link of each chain piece like you are opening a jump ring (Techniques) and attach one chain piece to each side of the paracord links **(j)**.

10 Open the last link in each chain and attach the magnetic clasp. Close the links.

f

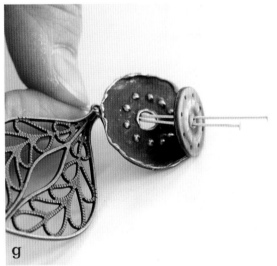

g

h

i

j

playful posies brooch

This project is especially exciting to me. My background is in sculpture, and I was thrilled when I discovered I could use paracord as a material to mold and sculpt. Paracord can be melted, frayed, stacked, and manipulated in so many intriguing ways. I love the idea of taking a material like paracord, that is so utilitarian and masculine, and transforming it into beautiful feminine little flower blooms.

1 Cut five 5-in. pieces of wire. Cut five 4-in. pieces of each color of paracord. Remove the white core, or kern, from each paracord piece.

2 Hold one paracord tube between your fingers. With the index finger of your other hand, press into the end of the tube **(a)**. While applying pressure, spin the tube between your fingers. This will cause the end of the tube to splay out.

3 When a lip has formed, hit the very edge with the lighter's flame **(b)**. Melting the edge will prevent the paracord

from continuing to fray. Repeat this process on one end of each paracord tube **(c)**.

4 Stick a scrap piece of wire through the un-flared end of a pink tube, bend the wire in half, feed the wire through the orange tube, and pull the wire ends to pull the pink tube in place. Remove the wire and repeat to get the orange tube inside of the green tube. Repeat this process for all the paracord tubes **(d, e, f)**.

5 Trim one tube grouping to about 2½ in., and hit the cut end with the lighter to stop the fraying. Make sure not to melt the tube closed. This first tube will be the core branch.

MATERIALS
- **5** 6mm vitrail medium Swarovski crystal marguerites
- 25 in. 22-gauge gunmetal wire
- 1 in. pin back finding
- 20 in. hot pink paracord 550
- 20 in. bright orange paracord 550
- 20 in. dark green paracord 550

TOOLS
- high-durability scissors
- chainnose pliers
- roundnose pliers
- wire snips
- butane lighter
- awl
- E6000 jewelry adhesive

a

b

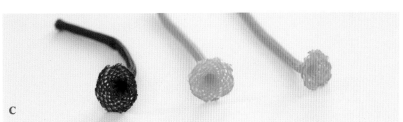

c

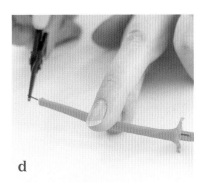

d

e

f

☙ tip

You may notice when buying paracord 550 that some feels thicker and more solid than others. The sturdier paracord has a tighter woven mantle. When coaxing the paracord to splay out, the tighter weave prevents the mantle from just falling apart.

g

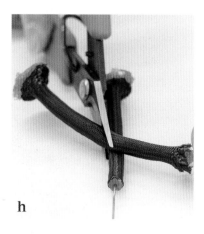

h

i

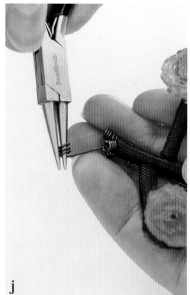

j

k

6 Using chainnose pliers fold the very end of a 5-in. piece of wire over, creating a stop at the end. String a crystal onto the wire, then string the wire down through the trimmed, melted tube **(g).**

7 To add more branches, place a tube group where you'd like a branch. Trim the tube to the appropriate length and at an angle that allows this second tube to lay flush to the first tube **(h)**. Melt the end of the second tube. String a wire through a crystal and down through the tube. Stab the wire end into the core branch where you'd like to add the second branch. You may need to use an awl to get the hole started. Feed the wire down through the core branch **(i)**.

8 Repeat step 7 until all five branches are connected.

9 Grasp the end of one wire with roundnose pliers. Turn the pliers to create a coil, and continue coiling until all the wire is used up and the branch is secure **(j).** Repeat for all the wires.

10 Glue the pin back to the back of the core branch **(k)**.

hemp, cotton & naturals

dye

wrap

knot

braid

stitch

sailor girl necklace

Hemp is a classic beginner material. Who hasn't tried a macramé project using hemp? But that's not all it's good for. Let's separate hemp from macramé and look at some of its other qualities. It's soft, flexible, strong, inexpensive, and easy to find. Most important for this project is that it is a natural fiber, and is super receptive to dyes.

a

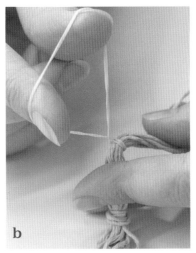

b

c

d

MATERIALS

- 34x52mm gold-plated vintage anchor (similar: etsy.com/shop/AZSupplies)
- 2½ in. gold-plated chain
- **2** 6mm gold-plated jump rings
- **2** 20-gauge gold-plated headpins
- 8 in. 22-gauge gold-plated wire
- **2** 9mm brass bullet casings (etsy.com/shop/designfrom-dixie or 8mm brass cord end from artbeads.com)
- 30 ft. 1.5mm hemp

TOOLS AND SUPPLIES

- permanent marker (blue or color of your choice)
- cord scissors
- chainnose pliers
- bentnose pliers
- roundnose pliers
- wire snips
- rubber bands
- nail
- hammer
- bench block

1 Cut 15 2-ft. pieces of hemp cord **(a)**. Cut two 4-in. pieces of wire.

2 Collect all the hemp pieces into a bundle. Bind one end with a rubber band. Moving along the bundle, wrap a rubber band approximately every inch **(b)**.

3 Using the permanent marker, color in all the spaces between rubber bands **(c)**.

4 Rinse the hemp in warm water until the water runs clear. Cut all the rubber bands off except those at either end of the bundle. Let dry **(d)**.

⑥ tip

If bullet casings are a bit too gruff for your style, replace them with something more feminine, like brass filigree cones. The anchor can be replaced with a pretty metal flower.

5 Wrap a wire around one end of the hemp bundle **(e)**. Use pliers to pull the wrapping tight **(f)**. Trim excess wire.

6 Trim off the scraggly ends of hemp and the last rubber band **(g)**. Repeat on the other end.

7 String a headpin up through the wire wrapping **(h)**. Repeat on the other side.

8 Make a hole in a bullet casing. Use a hammer and nail to pop out the primer (the little dimple) in the rear of the bullet casing **(i)**. Repeat with the second casing.

9 String the headpin at one end of the hemp bundle into a bullet casing and pull the hemp up inside the casing. Repeat on the other end **(j)**.

10 Make a double loop (Techniques) **(k)**. Repeat with the other end and casing.

11 Cut 2½ in. of chain. Use a jump ring to attach both ends of the chain to one bullet casing. Use a jump ring to attach the anchor to the other casing.

e

f

g

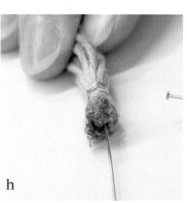

h

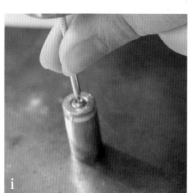

i

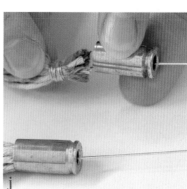

j

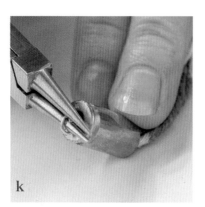

k

sea spray & lavender bracelet

When designing and working with cord, it can be difficult to locate the findings you want. It's not easy to find clasps and cord ends in the metal color you're looking for, not to mention in unique and trendy styles. So, get creative! Don't be afraid to get out some adhesive, combine a few different findings, and end up with something that's totally you. Try looking at what you've got differently—use a finding backwards, or make your clasp the focal piece.

MATERIALS

- 25x42mm antiqued brass filigree
- 20mm handmade lavender glass disk
- 12mm mother-of-pearl cabochon
- 7x13mm vintage brass fold-over clasp (similar: MissAshleyKate.com)
- **2** 19mm hefty antique brass jump rings
- 1 ft. 22-gauge antique bronze wire
- 18 ft. 1mm mint hemp

TOOLS AND SUPPLIES

- cord scissors
- chainnose pliers
- bentnose pliers
- wire snips
- rubber bands
- E6000 jewelry adhesive

1 Cut 18 12-in. pieces of hemp. Cut six 4-in. pieces of wire.

2 Divide the hemp into three groups. Bind each group using a rubber band. Braid each group **(a)** and bind the other end with a rubber band.

3 Apply a small amount of glue on one braid approximately ¼ in. from the rubber band. Fold the braid around a jump ring **(b)**.

4 Wrap a piece of wire three times around the braid where the glue is, to bind it in place **(c)**.

5 Trim the wire and the braid **(d)**.

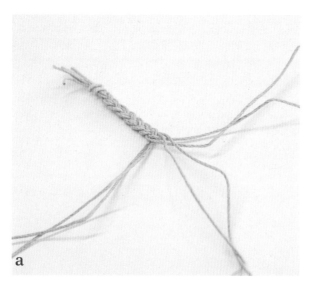

a

b

⑥ tip

Remember to clean components before gluing! This is especially important when gluing pieces that will be under high stress, like clasps. Vintage, glass, and natural components often come with a layer of oily, dusty residue. Simply wash the piece with a little dish soap and water.

c

d

e

f

6 Repeat steps 3 and 4 for the other braids, using the same jump ring. Repeat on the other end with a new jump ring. Make the braided section equal to the desired bracelet length less 1½ in. **(e)**.

7 Apply glue to the back side of the clasp and press it into the middle of the filigree **(f)**.

8 Glue the glass disk and mother-of-pearl cab to the other side of the filigree **(g)**.

9 Open the jump ring and attach the clasp loop **(h)**. Close the jump ring.

10 Fasten the bracelet by connecting the clasp to the other jump ring.

g

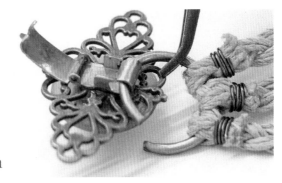

h

jute wrapped blooms

Natural fibers like jute have marvelous little fuzzies. Jewelry is very often composed of sleek components—think polished stone, glass, and metals. The jute in this project adds the tactile element of fuzz. Pair it with the elegance of Swarovski crystals for a interesting play of materials.

a

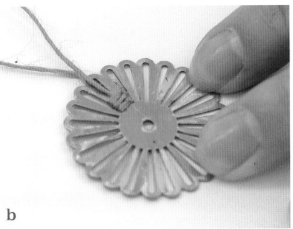

b

c

d

MATERIALS
- **3** 36mm vintage copper flowers (echoartworks.com)
- **3** 12mm golden Sahara Swarovski crystal sew-ons
- **4** 4mm antiqued copper jump rings
- 4 ft. 2mm purple leather lacing
- 16 in. open link chain (optional)
- 128 in. salmon thin jute
- 128 in. navy thin jute
- 128 in. olive thin jute

TOOLS AND SUPPLIES
- cord scissors
- chainnose pliers
- bentnose pliers
- Big Eye needle
- E6000 jewelry adhesive
- superglue pen

1 Cut 16 in. of salmon jute. Thread the Big Eye needle and wrap the jute once around two flower spokes, leaving a 3-in. tail **(a)**.

2 Fold the tail down and wrap over it **(b)**. Continue wrapping until the spokes are full **(c)**. Tie a double knot using the 3-in. tail and the working thread **(d)**. Apply a dab of superglue to the knot and trim.

⑥ tip
What is a sew-on crystal? It is a crystal in a setting. The setting has holes, allowing you to stitch the crystal onto a base. The prong setting gives the crystal a professional, finished look.

For a quick and easy finish, cut a 16–in. piece of chain and use the outer jump rings attached in step 7 to connect it to the focal piece.

e

f

3 Skip one flower spoke, and repeat steps 1 and 2 **(e)**.

4 Repeat step 3 until all the flower spokes are filled.

5 Apply E6000 jewelry adhesive to the back of one sew-on crystal. Press the sew-on into the middle of the copper flower **(f)**.

6 Repeat steps 1–5 to make a navy flower and an olive flower.

7 Attach the three flowers together using jump rings (Techniques) **(g)**. Attach a jump ring to each outer flower.

8 Cut two 2-ft. pieces of leather lacing. String each cord through a jump ring to complete the necklace. Wear the necklace with the cords doubled and tied in the back.

g

stitched earrings

Wrapping or stitching onto metal with cord is a simple way to add color and texture to metal components. The success of these earrings lies in the several contrasting elements: the dull brass paired with bright blue, the hard metal paired with soft cord, and the combination of very masculine cogs and gears embellished with traditionally feminine stitching.

MATERIALS

- **2** 25mm antiqued brass gears
- **2** 15mm antiqued brass cogs
- **2** 4mm antiqued brass jump rings
- pair of antiqued brass earring wires
- 13 ft. blue cotton cord

TOOLS

- cord scissors
- chainnose pliers
- bentnose pliers
- 1.8mm metal hole punch
- superglue pen

a

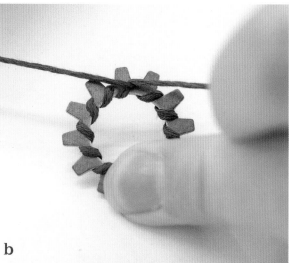

b

c

1 Cut 1 ft. of cord. String the cord through the middle of a gear, leave a 1½-in. tail, and wrap the cord once between each tooth **(a)**.

2 Once back at the beginning, twist the tail and the working cord, redirecting the working cord the other direction **(b)**.

3 Flip the gear over and wrap the cord from the outside to the inside (the cording will be making V shapes on the gear) **(c)**.

d

e

f

4 Once fully around, tie a double overhand knot using the tail and the working cord. Apply glue to the knot. Trim any remaining cord.

5 Using the metal punch, punch a hole in one of the gear teeth **(d)**.

6 Cut 6 in. of cord. Leave a 1½-in. tail and thread the cord (back to front) through one of the small holes in the cog and then thread the cord (front to back) through the big hole. Move to the next small hole and thread the cord (back to front) through it **(e)**. Repeat all the way around.

7 Using the tail and the working cord, tie a double overhand knot, apply glue, and trim the ends.

8 Attach the gear and cog together using a jump ring (Techniques) **(f)**.

9 Attach an earring wire to the top loop in the cog.

linear geometry necklace

Wrapped beads are not a new idea, but look how intriguing it is to let the bead underneath show through. Wrapping beads allows you to customize your own components. This piece uses lines as a design thread and plays with positive and negative space.

1 Cut 2 ft. of cord.

2 String the cord through a bead, leaving a 3-in. tail **(a)**. Wrap the cord around the bead 11 times **(b)**.

3 Tie a knot using the tail and the working cord **(c)**. Pull the ends tight, and pull the knot into the bead **(d)**.

4 Apply a small amount of glue to the knot. Trim the remaining cord.

MATERIALS

- **8** 14mm vintage steel gourd cages (echoartworks.com)
- **8** 10mm orange Lucite pony beads (MissAshleyKate.com)
- **8** 8mm faceted hematite rounds
- 6 in. 2mm dark silver-plated cable chain
- **8** 8mm heavy gauge silver-plated jump rings
- **2** 4mm gunmetal jump rings
- **8** 20-gauge silver-plated eyepins
- 9mm gunmetal trailer-hitch clasp
- 16 ft. purple cotton cord

TOOLS

- cord scissors
- chainnose pliers
- bentnose pliers
- roundnose pliers
- wire snips
- superglue gel

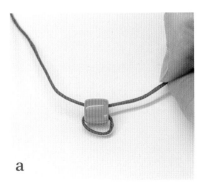

a

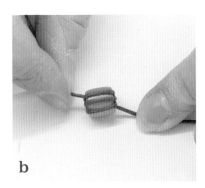

b

tip
When choosing glue for this project, choose a gel glue. Using the gel reduces dripping and spreading and makes a clean and attractive finished piece.

c

d

e

5 Open an eyepin and slide the loop of a cage on (Techniques). Close the eyepin and string it through the wrapped bead and a hematite round **(e)**. Make a wrapped loop (Techniques).

6 Repeat steps 1–3 to make eight links.

7 Using 8mm jump rings, attach the links together **(f)**.

8 Cut two 3-in. pieces of chain. Open the last link in a chain piece and attach it to the linked beads **(g)**. Repeat on the other end.

9 Attach one end of the chain to a clasp end using a 4mm jump ring. Repeat on the other end.

f

g

knots & baubles necklace

This project presents a modern twist on a classic knot. The monkey fist knot is traditionally very useful, as it can be used as an anchor, a weight, a weapon, and much more. It was originally made around a heavy rock or steel ball. This project makes a lightweight, dainty knot around a bead. This technique is an easy way to create your own beads and add new textural elements to any jewelry piece.

MATERIALS

- **4** 8mm faceted orange givre rounds
- **6** 4mm matte deep orange rounds
- **2** 4mm opaque pink faceted rounds
- **5** 6mm plastic rounds
- 18 in. dull silver cable chain 4x5mm
- **12** 22-gauge 2-in. gunmetal headpins
- 6mm silver jump ring
- **6** 4mm gunmetal jump rings
- 12mm lobster claw clasp
- 9 ft. orange 1mm cotton cord
- 6 ft. pink 1mm cotton cord

TOOLS

- cord scissors
- chainnose pliers
- roundnose pliers
- wire snips
- superglue gel
- Big Eye needle

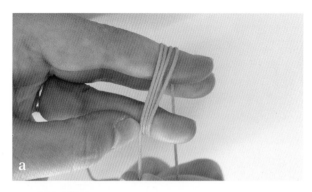

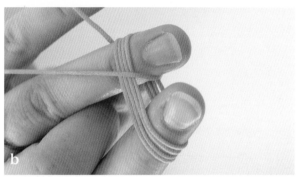

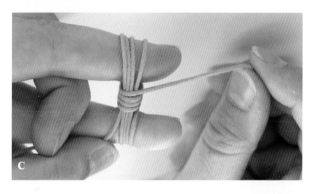

1 Cut three 3-ft. pieces of orange cord and two 3-ft. pieces of pink cord.

2 Starting with an orange cord, leave a 2-in. tail and wrap the cord four times around your index and ring fingers (**a**). Begin at your fingertips and wrap toward your palm.

3 Pull the cord between your two fingers so it rests on top of your ring finger (**b**).

4 Wrap the cord four times around the first set of wraps. This second set will fill in between your fingers, wrapping from ring finger to index finger (**c**).

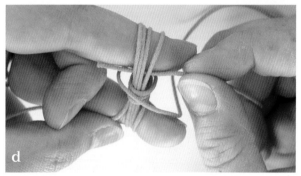

5 Feed the tail of the cord through the space between your index finger and the last wrap, towards your palm (**d**).

6 Very carefully pull the wrapping off your fingers. Hold onto the middle set of wraps (**e**).

7 Pull the working end around the back and feed it through the loop where your ring finger used to be. Pop the 6mm plastic bead into

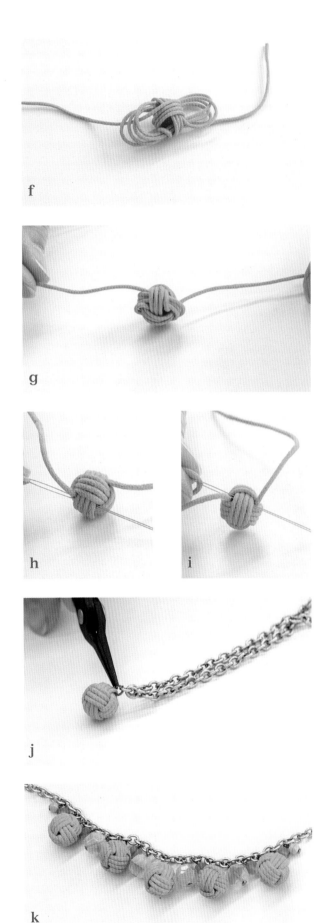

tip

Practice making your first monkey's fist with paracord. The larger, smoother cord is easier to see and allows you to smoothly tighten the knot, making the process more manageable.

the middle of the wrapping. Wrap three more times through the loops where your index and ring fingers were for a total of four wraps **(f)**.

8 Pull the tail you left at the beginning to start tightening the wrapping around the bead **(g)**. Tighten up each wrap in order and make sure all the wraps are in line.

9 Thread the Big Eye needle on one of the cord tails. Sew the tail under the wraps in front of it **(h)**. Repeat for the other tail, so both tails are coming out of the same spot **(i)**. Trim the tails and dab with superglue.

10 Repeat to make a total of three orange knots and two pink knots.

11 String an 8mm bead onto a headpin and make a simple loop above the bead (Techniques). Repeat with the remaining 8mm beads and all the 4mm beads.

12 Attach a jump ring to each monkey knot through one cord wrap (Techniques).

13 Attach an orange knot to the center of the 18-in. chain **(j)**.

14 On each side, skip one chain link and attach an orange givre bead. Continue skipping a link and adding dangles in this order: one orange matte round, one pink knot, one orange givre bead, one orange matte round, one orange knot, one orange matte round, and one opaque pink bead (Techniques) **(k)**.

15 Attach a 6mm jump ring to one end of the chain and a lobster claw clasp to the other using a 4mm jump ring.

f

g

h

i

j

k

sea siren necklace

This necklace references the nautical origins of the rope. You can envision big coils of this thick, twisted rope down at the docks. This necklace looks like a fisherman's rope washed ashore, tangled with tiny treasures. The larger surface of this rope makes it easy to embellish. Following the twist of the natural fibers, you can easily stitch chains and charms to the rope.

a

b

c

1 Cut two 2-ft. pieces of rope. Tie a loose overhand knot in one rope about 5½ in. from one end **(a)**.

2 String the 13mm rondelle until it's within the knot **(b)**.

3 String the untied rope through the knot, aligning its end with the short side of the tied rope **(c)**.

4 Cut 5 ft. of thread. Thread the needle with a double length of thread and knot the ends. Sew through the back of the untied rope, so the needle exits just below the loop of the tied rope **(d)**.

d

MATERIALS

- 13mm brass crystal rondelle with 6mm hole
- 10mm vintage brass starfish charm (similar: etsy.com/shop/brasskicker)
- 9mm vintage green crystal sew-on (similar: sewoncrystals.com)
- 8mm matte crystal teardrop
- **3** 4mm beige glass pearls
- 4mm opal with rosy wash Chinese crystal rondelle
- 2 in. 3mm green opal brass cup chain
- 4½ in. 3mm white opal brass cup chain
- 2 ft. 6mm hemp rope
- 2 15x20mm brass flower cones
- **2** 20-gauge 2-in. brass headpins
- 21mm gold-plated toggle clasp
- **2** 4mm brass jump rings
- 5 ft. off-white cotton/polyester sewing thread

TOOLS AND SUPPLIES

- scissors
- tape
- sewing needle
- wire snips
- chainnose pliers
- roundnose pliers
- E6000 jewelry adhesive

᎒ tip

Twisted rope like the one used in this project can easily unravel when cut. To prevent unraveling, decide where you need to cut, wrap tape around this point, and then cut straight through the tape. The rope will stay neat and tidy!

e

f

g

h

i

j

k

5 Stitch the green sew-on in place under the loop of the tied rope (**e**). Stitch the starfish charm in place under the sew-on and slightly to the left (**f**). Move slightly to the right of the charm and stitch on the pearl, the crystal, and the teardrop bead. On the reverse side, make a few stitches through the tied and untied ropes to hold them all together and in place.

6 Cut 2 in. of white opal cup chain and 4½ in. of green opal cup chain. Place the white opal chain under the teardrop on the left rope. Stitch around the chain under the first cup of the chain to hold it in place. Wrap the chain around the rope, following the twist of the rope. Stitch into the core of the rope and then tack the chain in place. Repeat for the green opal cup chain, attaching it around the right rope (**g**).

7 Place the whole piece flat on the table. Adjust the ropes so the left rope lays snugly below the right rope. Trim the rope ends evenly (**h**).

8 Apply E6000 jewelry adhesive to the rope ends. Make sure to really saturate the rope and get glue into the rope's center (**i**). You may want to wear gloves or use an applicator.

9 String a glass pearl and a flower cone on a headpin. Apply more glue and press a rope end into a flower cone (**j**). Repeat on the other end. Make a wrapped loop with each headpin (Techniques).

10 Attach a toggle clasp half to each wrapped loop using a 4mm jump ring (**k**) (Techniques).

leather

flowers

stamp

knot

cut

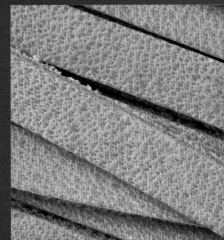

stack

heat form

charm & flare bracelet

Leather lacing is extremely strong. There are all kinds of great colors and thicknesses on the market today. Lacing is easy to punch through and makes a great building base for this jangling charm bracelet.

1 Using the metal punch, punch a hole at each end of each piece of leather **(a)**.

2 Roughly 1 in. from the end of the olive leather, punch a second hole; continue punching holes roughly every inch until there are 10 holes in the olive leather (including the holes already punched at each end).

3 Roughly ½ in. from the end, punch a second hole in the mauve leather. Punch the remaining holes roughly 1 in. apart until there are 10 holes in the leather (including the holes already punched at each end).

4 Add the bead loops to the olive leather: String a 20-gauge headpin from back to front through the second hole in the leather. String a teal irregular-cut bicone **(b)**. Make a simple loop (Techniques) **(c)**. Continue attaching beads to the leather. Use this pattern: teal irregular-cut bicone (just added), olive rondelle, purple copper washed round, matte teal round, olive jade round, and purple rondelle **(d)**.

MATERIALS

- **2** 7mm irregular-cut teal glass bicones
- **2** 6mm purple copper washed glass rounds
- **2** 6mm faceted olive jade rounds
- **2** 5mm olive opal czech glass rondelles
- **2** 5mm matte teal glass rounds
- **2** 4.5mm purple faceted glass rondelles
- **36** 4mm antique gold crystal rondelles
- **12** 2-in. 20-gauge brass headpins
- **36** 2-in. 24-gauge brass headpins
- **2** 8mm brass hefty jump rings
- 22mm brass S hook
- 6¾ in. 4.7mm mauve leather lacing
- 6¾ in. 4.7mm olive leather lacing

TOOLS

- cord scissors
- chainnose pliers
- bentnose pliers
- roundnose pliers
- wire snips
- 1.8mm metal punch

⑥ tip

Use an assembly-line method for making your crystal dangles. Make the first bend of your wrapped loop on all the headpins, then the second to all the headpins, etc. This practice will greatly improve your efficiency.

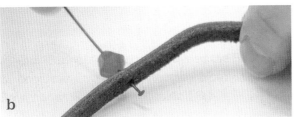

a

b

c

d

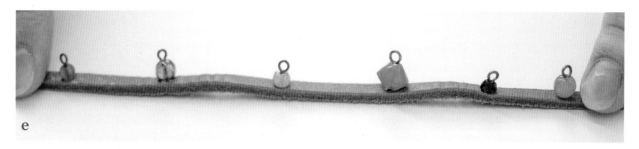

e

f

g

5 Repeat this same process with the mauve leather. Attach the beads in this order: olive jade round, purple rondelle, teal irregular-cut bicone, olive rondelle, purple copper washed round, and matte teal round **(e)**.

6 Make 36 crystal dangles: String a crystal on a 24-gauge headpin and make a wrapped loop (Techniques) **(f)**.

7 Attach three crystal dangles to each bead loop: Open the bead loop, slide on three dangles, and close the loop **(g)**.

8 Position the hole at the end of the mauve leather over the hole at the end of the olive leather. Connect a jump ring through the holes (Techniques) **(h)**. At the other end, position the olive leather on top of the mauve and connect a jump ring through the holes. Attach the "S" hook clasp though the jump rings.

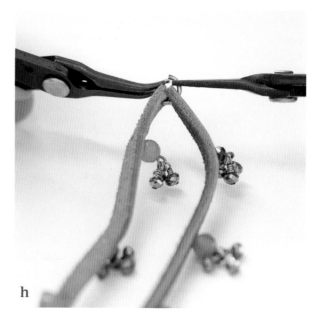

h

diamond duster earrings

Leather provides the perfect surface to embellish. When I discovered a rubber-stamping ink product called StazOn, I was more than excited. It allows you to stamp on almost any material including plastic, metal, and polymer clay. You can use store-bought stamps or get creative and make some of your own!

MATERIALS

- new or recycled black leather scraps
- pair of gold-plated earring wires
- **2** 6mm gold-plated jump rings

TOOLS AND SUPPLIES

- StazOn ink kit, metallic gold
- quilt square rubber stamp
- feather or pine sprig stamp
- fabric scissors
- chainnose pliers
- bentnose pliers
- 1.8mm metal hole punch

1 Prepare the ink pad according to the instructions in the kit.

2 Stamp two squares and two feathers onto the black leather. Let dry **(a)**.

3 Cut out the squares and the feathers using sharp fabric scissors **(b)**.

4 Punch a hole at the end of a feather's stem **(c)**. Repeat with the other feather.

a

b

c

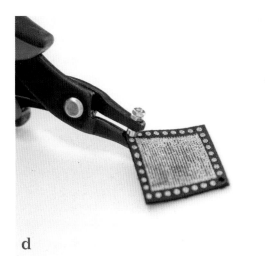

d

⑥ tip
StazOn comes in a wide variety of colors. When using a dark-colored leather, I have found that the metallic inks are best. They are more opaque than the other colors and therefore can still be seen on the dark leather background.

e

f

5 Punch a hole in one of the corners of a square **(d)**. Punch another hole in the corner opposite the first hole. Repeat with the other square.

6 Attach one feather and one square together using a jump ring (Techniques) **(e)**. Repeat with the other feather and square.

7 Attach an earring wire to each square (Techniques) **(f)**.

twist & tangle necklace

I was determined to do something new with leather cording because I have seen it almost exclusively used as a pendant cord. Leather cord is strong, flexible, and handsome. The biggest obstacle when using leather cord is finding gorgeous beads that have large enough holes to accommodate the cord. This project provides an easy alternative to stringing and allows you to use beads with any size hole.

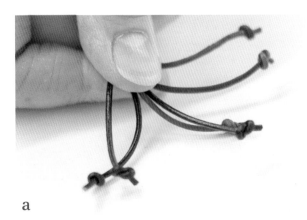

a

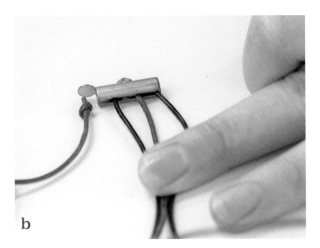

b

c

MATERIALS

- **7** 13x19mm faceted quartz nuggets
- **7** 8mm gold disk charms
- **2** 6x20mm brass ball chain clamps
- **6** 4mm light Colorado topaz
  Swarovski crystal flat backs
- 1 ft. 6mm brass double-link chain
- **7** 20-gauge gold-plated eyepins
- 15mm lobster claw clasp
- 4mm gold-plated hefty jump ring
- 42 in. 1.5mm black leather cord
- 56 in. 1.5mm brown leather cord

TOOLS AND SUPPLIES

- cord scissors
- chainnose pliers
- bentnose pliers
- roundnose pliers
- wire snips
- crystal applicator
- E6000 jewelry adhesive

1 Cut four 14-in. pieces of brown leather cord and three 14-in. pieces of black leather cord. Tie a knot at one end of every cord and trim the leather so the knot is at the very end **(a)**.

2 Slide the knots into the chain clamp. Start with a brown cord and alternate brown and black **(b)**.

3 Bend the open side of the chain clamp closed **(c)**.

d

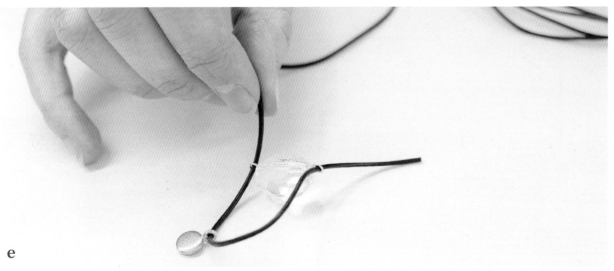

e

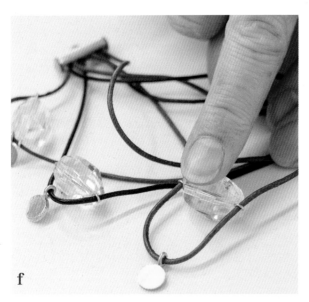

f

4 String a quartz nugget onto an eyepin. Make a simple loop above the stone (Techniques) **(d)**. Repeat with the remaining nuggets.

5 String a leather cord through a quartz link loop. String one gold disk charm. String the leather cord through the remaining loop of the quartz link **(e)**.

6 Repeat step 4, adding one quartz link and one gold disk charm to each leather cord **(f)**.

7 Purposefully tangle and move the cords and links around until everything lies in a pleasing way **(g)**.

8 Tie a knot at the end of each cord and trim any remaining cord. Slide all the knots into a chain clamp and close the clamp **(h)**.

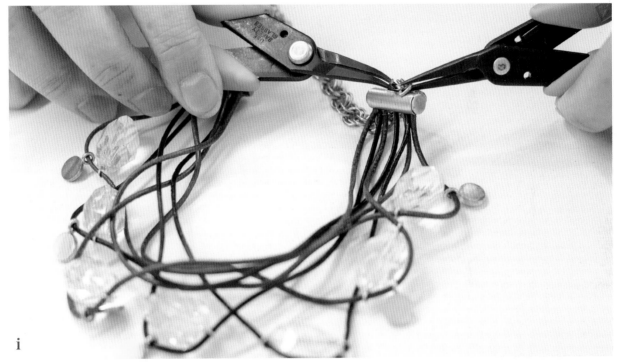

9 Cut two 6-in. pieces of chain. Open the end links of one chain and attach the chain to the chain clamp (Techniques). Repeat with the other chain and the other chain clamp **(i)**.

10 Attach the lobster claw clasp to one end of the chain with a 4mm jump ring.

11 Apply a tiny amount of glue to each chain clamp. Use the crystal applicator to pick up and place three crystals on each chain clamp **(j)**.

ombré pom-pom necklace

Leather is lightweight, flexible, and can add fabulous volume to jewelry. This project uses repetition and fringe to create movement and whimsy. The crystal rondelles provide a flash of sparkle and complete the statement.

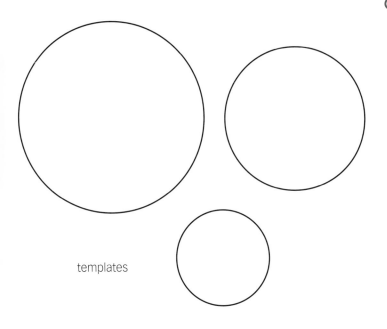

templates

a

b

MATERIALS

- 2½–2¼ ft. recycled brown suede scraps
- 2x2 ft. recycled burgundy/purple suede scraps
- 1½x1½ ft. recycled red suede scraps. (New leather: tandyleatherfactory.com, recycled leather: MissAshleyKate.com, Leather scrap grab bags: A. C. Moore or Michaels)
- **14** 10mm vintage copper 5-petal flowers (echoartworks.com)
- **7** 12mm copper crystal rondelles
- **14** 6mm metallic iris crystal rounds
- **7** 20-gauge antiqued copper eyepins
- 2 ft. 13x7x2mm antiqued copper large ovals and cable chain
- 15mm antique copper toggle

TOOLS

- sharp fabric scissors
- high-durability scissors
- chainnose pliers
- bentnose pliers
- roundnose pliers
- wire snips
- 2-in. jar lid (or other found object)
- ½-in. diameter button (or other found object)
- 1-in. diameter button (or other found object)

1 Trace the circles onto the suede: Trace 14 2-in. circles on the brown suede, 14 1½-in. circles on the burgundy suede, and 14 1-in. circles on the red suede **(a)**. Using sharp fabric scissors, cut out all the circles.

2 Stack the circles by size. Using high-durability scissors, make small cuts into the circles all the way around **(b)**.

⑥ **tip**
You do not need solid leather pieces; you can work from scraps.

c

d

e

3 Place the circles in stacks of three: one large, one medium, and one small. Using an awl, poke a hole through the middle of a stack **(c)**.

4 Using chainnose pliers, bend the petals of all the copper flowers. Bend them up so they form a cup- or cone-like shape **(d)**.

5 On an eyepin, string components in this order: one 6mm crystal round, one 2-in. circle, one 1½-in. circle, one 1-in. circle, one copper flower (front to back), one copper crystal rondelle, one copper flower (back to front), one 1-in. circle, one 1½-in. circle, one 2-in. circle, and one 6mm crystal round **(e)**. Turn a simple loop (Techniques) to complete the link **(f)**. Repeat to make seven pom-pom links.

f

g

h

i

6 Disassemble the chain to get six free oval links **(g)**. Use the oval links to attach all the pom-pom links together (Techniques) **(h)**.

7 Cut two 6-in. pieces of chain. Attach one chain length to each end of the pom-pom links using an oval chain link **(i)**.

8 Open the last link of each chain piece (Techniques) and attach half the toggle clasp to each chain end.

6 tip

Instead of using paper templates, I prefer found objects. Buttons and jar lids work great for tracing—they are stiffer than paper and much easier to trace around.

plum flower necklace or wrap bracelet

Leather flowers are a blast to make. Experimenting with size, shape, color, and heat forming can result in a bouquet of options. This project uses recycled leather. I collect leather goods from thrift shops and repurpose them into happy jewelry. When choosing your leather, lower quality actually works better. Look for bonded leather or leather that has a plastic/polyurethane skin. The plastic bonding curls when exposed to heat, creating cute, little cupped petals.

templates

MATERIALS

- **3** 12mm 24k plated vintage 5-petal flowers (similar: etsy.com/shop/VintageBeadCache)
- **15** 10mm olive jade rounds
- **15** 7mm olive freshwater pearls
- **3** 6mm Swarovski vitrail medium crystal margaritas
- **3** 8mm gold-plated bead caps
- **33** 24-gauge brass headpins
- 6¾ in. (35 links) antique brass cable chain (open link)
- 3 ft. brown leather lacing
- 12x12 in. recycled leather (does not have to be single piece. New leather: tandyleatherfactory.com, recycled leather: MissAshleyKate.com)

TOOLS AND SUPPLIES

- chainnose pliers
- bentnose pliers
- roundnose pliers
- wire snips
- sharp fabric scissors
- awl
- tea candle

1 Cut the recycled leather into nine squares: three 1x1 in., three 1¼x1¼ in., and three 1½x1½ in. (you may want to cut a few extra for practice). Cut the squares into five-petal flowers (see templates). Use sharp fabric scissors **(a)**.

2 Light the tea candle. Pinch one of the flower petals between your fingers and press the tip of the petal up and towards your fingers. This action should cause the petal to cup. Rotate the petal near the flame to provide even heat contact until the petal begins to curl up and cup **(b)**. Repeat for all the petals.

a

b

3 Stack the flowers into three stacks, with the biggest flower in the back, then the medium, and then the small. Use an awl to poke a hole through each stack of flowers. String flower components onto a headpin in this order: one crystal margarita, one gold flower, one small leather flower, one medium leather flower, one large leather flower, and one gold bead cap **(c)**. Make a wrapped loop (Techniques) **(d)**. Repeat with the other two flower stacks.

4 String a pearl on a headpin and make a wrapped loop (Techniques) in this manner **(e)**. Make all the olive pearls and olive jade rounds into dangles.

5 Cut 6¾ in. of chain (35 chain links). Skip the first chain link, open the second (Techniques), and string one pearl dangle **(f)**. On the next link add a jade dangle. Repeat this pattern until eight dangles have been attached.

6 After the eighth dangle, attach one leather flower dangle to the link **(g)**.

7 Attach seven bead dangles, a flower dangle, seven bead dangles, a flower dangle, and eight bead dangles **(h)**.

8 String the leather lacing through the last chain link on each side of the chain.

c

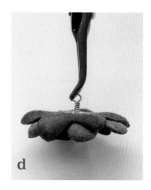
d

e

f

g

☙ tip To wear as a necklace, slip over your head and tie a bow in the leather. To wear as a bracelet, slip on to your wrist, wrap the leather ends around your wrist, and tie a bow.

h

ribbon & lace

embellish

weave

wrap

stack

drape

lacy bloom bracelet

Lace is pretty, dainty, and intricate. Lace is great for embellishment and because of its loopy design it works easily into beading and jewelry making. Think of each lace loop as a bead or something to attach a bead to. It opens up many design possibilities.

1 Trim the lace to the length of the cup chain. Cut 18 in. of waxed linen.

3 Tie the end of the linen in a double overhand knot around the base of the clasp loop **(a)**.

4 Thread the needle with the waxed linen. Align the lace end with the cup chain end that the linen is tied to. Sew through the first sturdy hole in the lace from front to back **(b)**.

5 Pull the waxed linen behind the bracelet in front of the first pearl cup. Sew up through the loop that has just been formed **(c)**. Sew from front to back through the lace hole that lines up with the space between the next two pearl cups **(d)**. Place the cord behind the bracelet between the two pearl cups, and sew up through the loop that has just been formed **(e)**. Continue until you reach the end of the bracelet. Tie off the waxed linen to the base of the clasp loop and trim.

MATERIALS

- 34mm four-petal brass flower (similar: kabeladesign.com)
- 10mm square white opal volcano Swarovski sew-on crystal
- 8 in. antique bronze 22-gauge wire
- prefinished brass pearl cup chain bracelet
- 1 yd. dark teal waxed linen
- 1 ft. mint cotton lace trim

TOOLS

- scissors
- Big Eye needle
- chainnose pliers
- roundnose pliers
- wire snips

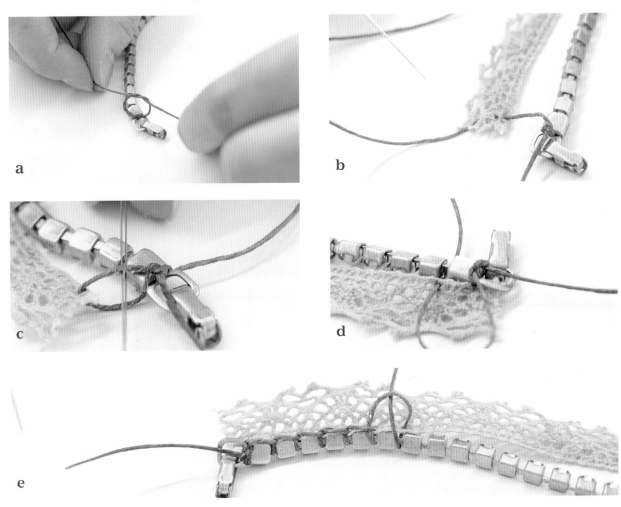

a

b

c

d

e

f

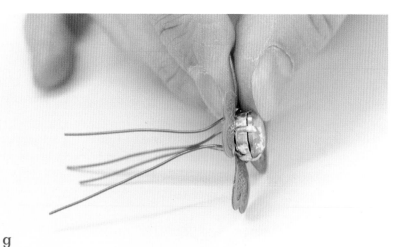

g

h

i

6 Cut two 4-in. pieces of bronze wire. Center the crystal sew-ons on the wires. Bend each wire to a 90-degree angle so all the wire tails point straight back from the crystal **(f)**.

7 String the wires into the spaces between the petals of the brass flower. Bend and pull the wires until the crystal fits snugly against the flower **(g)**. Bend one set of wires up against the back of the flower. Wrap the unbent wires twice around the bent wires **(h)**. Trim the tails of the wrapping wires.

8 With the remaining wires, begin making a wrapped loop (Techniques). Before completing the wrapped loop, slide it onto the bracelet, wrap it closed **(i)**, and trim any remaining wire.

pretty party pin

Ribbons! There are so many pretty ribbons, but have you ever noticed the interesting patterns and colors on the reverse side of ribbon? This project is glitzy, playful, and all about fun! There are no right or wrong answers in jewelry making, so just make happy jewelry!

MATERIALS

- 44mm vintage silver-plated filigree (similar: etsy.com/shop/SmartParts)
- 30mm vintage gunmetal 5-petal flower (similar: echoartworks.com)
- 10x15mm vintage brass cone (echoartworks.com)
- enameled headpin, teal
- enameled headpin, lime
- enameled headpin, cobalt (JenniferFahnestock.com)
- 20-gauge silver-plated eyepin
- silver-plated pin back
- 8¼x1 in. woven brocade ribbon
- 5 in. green sparkle ribbon

TOOLS AND SUPPLIES

- sharp fabric scissors
- chainnose pliers
- roundnose pliers
- wire snips
- E6000 jewelry adhesive

1 Cut three 2¾-in. pieces of brocade lace and one 5-in. piece of sparkle ribbon. Fray the ends of the brocade ribbon **(a)**.

2 Trim the enameled headpins: Cut one to ¾ in., one to 1 in., and one to 1¼ in. Turn loops at the end of each headpin (Techniques). Open an eyepin, string all of the headpin loops, and close the eyepin (Techniques) **(b)**.

3 Layer and fan all the brocade ribbons on top of each other (reverse side up) so they resemble an asterisk. Fold the sparkle ribbon ends in toward the middle of the ribbon so the ends overlap slightly. Place the sparkle ribbon on top of the brocade **(c)**.

4 String components onto the decorated eyepin in this order: brass cone, gunmetal flower, the middle of the sparkle ribbon, the middle of the brocade ribbons, and the middle of the filigree **(d)**. Turn a double loop in the eyepin (Techniques). Apply glue to the double loop **(e)**.

5 Glue the pin back to the top portion of the filigree component **(f)**.

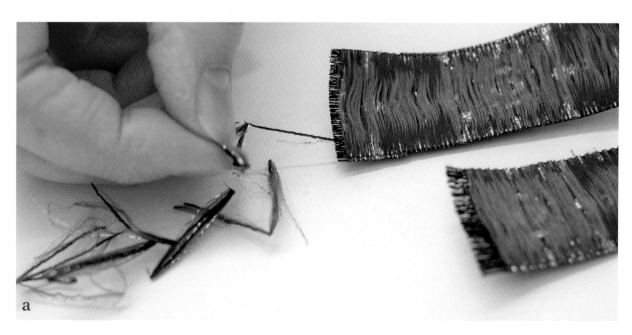

a

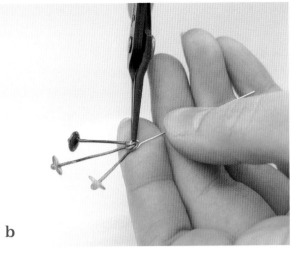

b

c

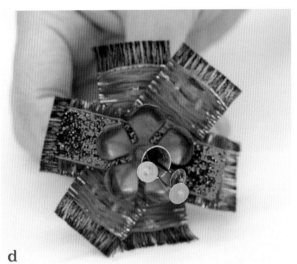

d

e

f

☾ tip

After you've opened your tube of glue, store it in a sealed plastic bag. This will greatly extend the life of your glue.

ribbon-wrapped mandala

There are so many types of ribbon—it comes in all different colors, sizes, and materials. This project uses silk embroidery ribbon. It is very thin and delicate. It works wonderfully in jewelry design because it is thin enough to fit through most beads. This project uses a technique that is akin to a peyote stitch/crochet hybrid.

MATERIALS

- 18mm perforated coin
- **21** 4mm opal gold-washed crystal rondelles
- **21** 4mm tanzanite satin crystal rondelles
- 18 in. 6x8mm oval cable chain (open link)
- 12mm lobster claw clasp
- 2 ft. light olive silk embroidery ribbon
- 2 ft. lavender silk embroidery ribbon

TOOLS

- scissors
- Big Eye needle
- chainnose pliers
- bentnose pliers
- wire snips

a

b

1 Cut 2 ft. of each ribbon color.

2 Thread the needle with the olive ribbon. Leaving a 3-in. tail, sew (from back to front) through one of the holes in the coin **(a)**. String an opal crystal rondelle. Sew through the next hole in the coin **(b)**. Sew from front to back through the space to the right of the crystal, between the coin and the ribbon **(c)**.

c

d

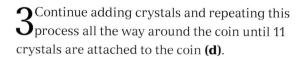

3 Continue adding crystals and repeating this process all the way around the coin until 11 crystals are attached to the coin **(d)**.

4 When adding the last crystal, sew back to front through the first crystal's loop **(e)**.

5 Flip the coin over and tie a double knot, using the 3-in. tail and the working ribbon **(f)**.

6 String a crystal and sew through the hole in the first attached crystal **(g)**.

e

f

g

h

i

j

7 String another crystal and sew through the next attached crystal. Repeat until you're back at the beginning again. Tie a double knot **(h)** and trim the left over ribbon.

8 Thread the needle with lavender ribbon. Sew back to front between two attached crystals **(i)**.

9 String a crystal and sew back to front through the space to the right of the next crystal. Sew from front to back through the space to the right of the crystal. Repeat **(j)** completely around the coin. Tie a knot and trim the ribbon.

10 Cut two 9-in. pieces of chain. Open an end link of one chain piece and attach it to one of the coin's spokes. Skip three spokes and attach an end link of the other chain piece **(k)**.

11 Open the last link of one chain piece and attach the lobster claw clasp.

k

courtly velvet wristlet

Securing a bracelet by tying an adorable little bow is so cute, but tying that bow with one hand can be quite the feat! The design of this wristlet helps combat the awkwardness of tying on a bracelet. One of the strands is elastic, which holds the wristlet in place while you tie the bow. Using velvet ribbon adds warmth and luxury to this simple piece.

a

b

c

MATERIALS

- 22mm gray metallic vintage square glass two-hole sew-on crystal (similar: etsy.com/shop/HansonStoneVintage)
- 13mm gray metallic vintage round glass two-hole sew-on crystal (alternate: etsy.com/shop/HansonStoneVintage)
- **23** 7mm apatite nuggets
- 19 in. 9mm magenta velvet polyester ribbon
- 6 in. antique brass 10x12mm double-link curb chain
- 2 ft. Opelon stretch cord

TOOLS

- scissors
- Big Eye needle
- chainnose pliers
- roundnose pliers
- wire snips
- butane lighter
- clear nail polish

1 Cut 6 in. (22 links) of chain. Cut 19 in. of velvet ribbon.

2 Leave a 6½-in. tail and weave the ribbon back to front through the chain links **(a)**.

3 Cut 2 ft. of stretch cord and thread the Big Eye needle with the cord. String the beads in this order: 22 apatite stones, round sew-on, an apatite stone, and square sew-on **(b)**. String the stretch cord through all the beads again; doubling the stretch cord greatly strengthens the bracelet. Tie a double knot in the stretch cord and dab with clear nail polish.

4 Place the square sew-on on top of the ribbon tail, right where it exits the last chain link **(c)**.

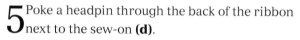

5 Poke a headpin through the back of the ribbon next to the sew-on **(d)**.

6 String the headpin through the unoccupied hole in the sew-on. Poke the headpin through the ribbon (front to back) as it exits the sew-on, and through the ribbon again from back to front (akin to making one stitch in the ribbon) **(e)**.

7 Trim the headpin to ¼ in. and make a simple loop **(f)** (Techniques). Open the loop and attach it to the last chain link (Techniques).

8 Repeat on the other end of the chain, using the round sew-on.

9 Trim away any fraying in the velvet, and lightly melt the ends with the lighter to prevent any future fraying.

10 To wear, slip the bracelet on your wrist and tie a bow.

⚲ tip
After tying off your stretch cord, always dab the knot with clear nail polish. The polish bonds the knot and prevents it from slipping. Steer clear of cyanoacrylates (superglues); they can actually eat through the elastic.

fringy fiesta necklace

I have always been drawn to trim, fringe, and all kinds of notions. I always think I'll get into sewing one day, but the truth is I'm just not very good at it. Whenever I do sit down to sew something it just doesn't hold my attention. This project allows you to use all those awesome sewing notions in jewelry design. Show off all that quirky, bold, and colorful yardage. Add a few stellar artist beads, and you've got quite the conversation piece.

MATERIALS

- 1 ft. yellow trim
- 1 ft. lilac trim
- 1 ft. orange and teal trim
- 1 ft. red trim
- **2** 30mm lampworked orange swirl disks (JenniferFahnestock.com)
- **2** 15mm vintage turquoise crystal components (similar: etsy.com/shop/oritdotan)
- **2** 8mm green round two-hole nail heads
- 8½ in. silver-plated 4mm cable chain (open link)
- 2 ft. 26-gauge silver-plated wire
- 10mm round silver-plated magnetic clasp

TOOLS

- sharp fabric scissors
- chainnose pliers
- bentnose pliers
- roundnose pliers
- wire snips

a

b

1 Cut six 4-in. pieces of 26-gauge wire. Gather the ends of all four pieces of trim together. Using a 4-in. piece of wire, bind the trim together **(a)**.

2 Adjust the drape of the four pieces of trim. Maneuver until they lay nicely and are aesthetically pleasing. Trim to your desired length. The pieces will roughly be 8½ in., 10½ in., 11½ in., and 12½ in. **(b)**. Gather the remaining ends of trim together. Using a 4-in. piece of wire, bind the trim together.

3 String a 4-in. piece of wire through each hole in a nail head. Bend the wires back 90 degrees **(c)**.

4 String the four wire ends through a crystal component and then through the hole in a lampworked disk **(d)**.

5 Place one bound end of the trim between the two sets of wire coming from the lampworked disk **(e)**.

6 Bend the set of wire that is between the trim up and over the binding on the trim. Wrap this set of wires around the other set three times and trim the excess wrapping wire **(f)**.

7 Make a wrapped loop with the other set of wires (Techniques) **(g)**. Cut excess wire. Repeat on the other end of the trim.

8 Cut two 4¼-in. pieces of chain. Open the last link of one chain piece (Techniques) and connect it to one of the wrapped loops **(h)**. Repeat with the remaining chain piece and wrapped loop.

9 Open the last link of each chain piece (Techniques) and attach the magnetic clasp.

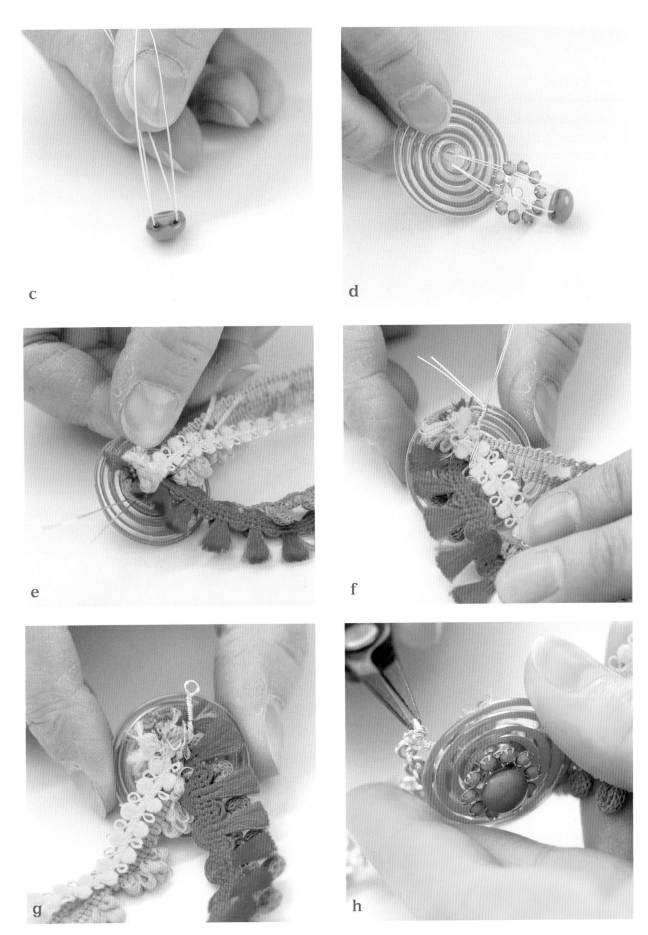

c

d

e

f

g

h

hoopla la lace earrings

Lace doesn't have to look dowdy or old fashioned. These earrings give classic cream lace a modern twist. This is a simple project that is quick to make and has many design alternatives.

1 Cut a 4-in. piece of lace. Apply a small amount of glue to the ends of the lace to keep it from fraying **(a)**.

2 Weave the hoop into the lace: String the hoop front to back through the first sturdy hole in the lace **(b)**. String the hoop through the second hole front to back. Continue weaving the hoop into the lace, always from front to back **(c, d)**.

MATERIALS

- 8 in. ½-in. wide cream lace
- 1 ft. yellow waxed linen
- 1 ft. turquoise waxed linen
- **2** 30mm gold-plated hoops

TOOLS AND SUPPLIES

- sharp fabric scissors
- cord scissors
- chainnose pliers
- white school glue

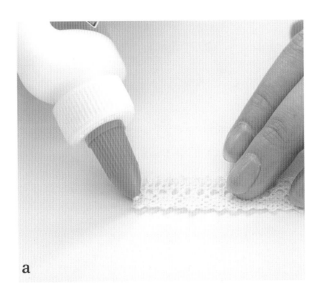

a

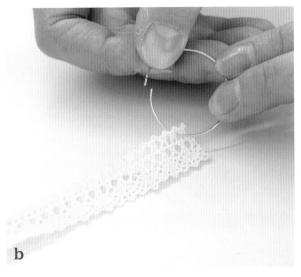

b

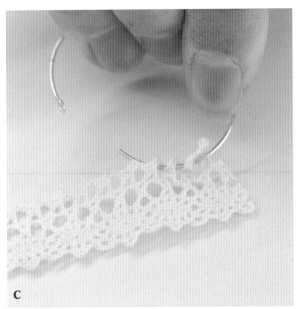

c

d

3 Cut a 6-in. piece each of yellow and turquoise waxed linen. Weave the turquoise linen through the line of bigger hole in the lace **(e)**.

4 Weave the yellow linen through the same path but in the opposite way **(f)** (where the turquoise goes under the yellow goes over). Trim the ends of the waxed linen so they are flush to the lace.

5 Using chainnose pliers, make a right-angle bend at the very end of the hoop to create a lock **(g)**.

6 Make a small dish of school glue diluted in equal parts with water. Dip the lace into the mixture **(h)**. Dab off excess glue and let dry on a flat surface.

7 Make a second earring.

e

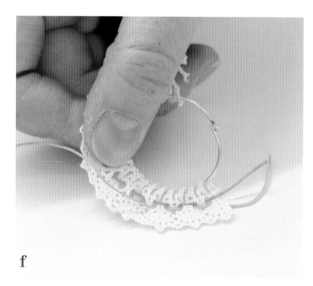

f

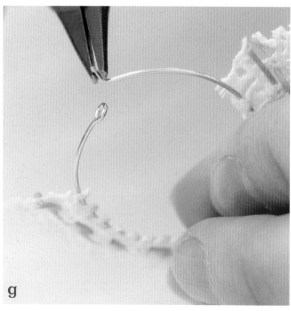

g

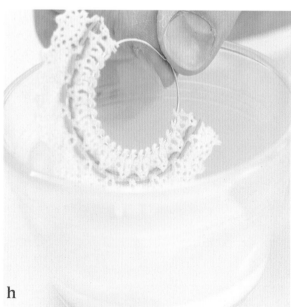

h

tropical woven bib necklace

Using different colored ribbons and alternating hitch knots creates a colorful striped necklace.
The shape of the necklace is formed by connecting and separating the two sets of knots. This
technique is a bit time-consuming but it's straightforward. Once you've grasped the concept,
you can design your own shapes and movement. The finished necklace is big and bold yet
lightweight and airy.

MATERIALS

- 11x27mm matte petrol green glass rice bead
- **2** 10x12mm matte olivine glass teardrop
- **2** 6mm matte pale blue opal glass round
- **2** 8x17x19mm gunmetal flat cones
- **5** 20-gauge 2-in. gunmetal eyepins
- 12mm gunmetal lobster claw clasp
- 8 in. 20-gauge gunmetal wire
- 6 in. 6mm gunmetal cable chain
- 2 yds. lime green paracord 550
- 11 ft. yellow ⅛-in. polyester ribbon
- 11 ft. lime green ⅛-in. polyester ribbon
- 22 ft. teal ⅛-in. polyester ribbon

TOOLS AND SUPPLIES

- high-durability scissors
- chainnose pliers
- roundnose pliers
- wire snips
- butane lighter
- E6000 jewelry adhesive
- tape

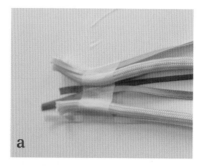

a

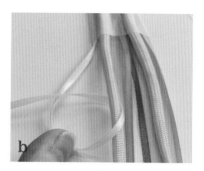

b

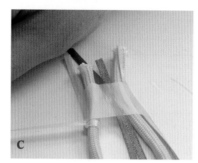

c

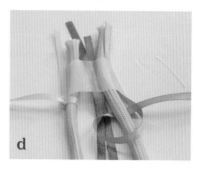

d

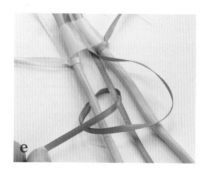

e

f

1 Cut two 11-ft. pieces of teal ribbon. Cut two 3-ft. pieces of green paracord. Tape down the ends of the cords in this order: yellow ribbon, paracord, teal ribbon, teal ribbon, paracord, and green ribbon **(a)**.

2 Place the yellow ribbon (left to right) over the left side paracord, leaving a loop to the left (the ribbon and the paracord should look like the number 4). Feed the ribbon under the paracord and up through the ribbon/"4" loop **(b)**. Pull up and to the left to tighten **(c)**. This is called a hitch knot.

3 Place the green ribbon (right to left) over the right side paracord, leaving a loop to the right. Feed the ribbon under the paracord and up through the ribbon loop. Pull up to the right to tighten **(d)**.

4 Place the left side teal ribbon over the left side paracord (right to left) leaving a loop to the right. Feed the ribbon under the right side teal ribbon and the left side paracord and up through the ribbon loop. Make sure to capture the other teal ribbon; it is what will keep the two sides together **(e)**. Pull up to the right to tighten.

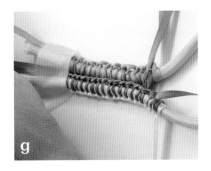

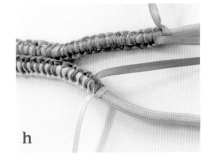

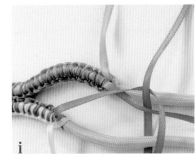

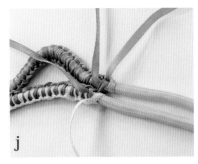

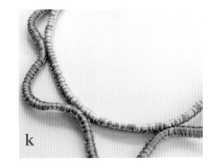

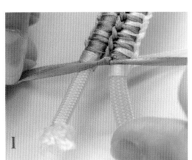

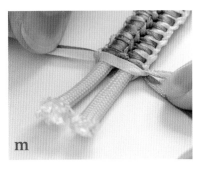

♭ tip

Working with long lengths of ribbon or cord can be a real headache. Wrap up the extra length and secure it with a rubber band. As you work, let out more length from under the rubber band.

5 Place the right side teal ribbon (working left to right) over the right side paracord, leaving a loop to the left. Feed the ribbon under the paracord and up through the ribbon loop **(f)**. Pull up to the left to tighten.

6 The design is made with a series of hitch knots around a left paracord and a right paracord. The two are joined together by catching the right side's teal ribbon in the left side's teal knot. The pattern is: outside left yellow, outside right green, inside left teal, and inside right teal. Repeat until the 16th green knot.

7 For the next inside left teal knot, don't catch the right side teal in the knot. The two sets will split apart into a yellow side and a green side **(g)**.

8 Continue tying knots until the eighth yellow knot on the yellow side and the 15th green knot on the green side **(h)**.

9 Bring the two sides back together. The next knot will be the left side teal—catch the right side teal in this knot **(i, j)**. Continue tying knots until the fifth set of yellow and green.

10 Continue tying in these increments **(k)**:
Apart: 16 yellow and 25 green
Together: Set of five yellow and green
Apart: 22 yellow and 29 green
Together: Set of five yellow and green
Apart: 16 yellow and 25 green
Together: Set of five yellow and green
Apart: Eight yellow and 15 green
Together: Set of 16 yellow and green

11 Tie off the ribbons: Tie a double knot in the two teal ribbons **(l)**. Tie a double knot with the yellow and green ribbons, tucking the teal tails into the double knot. Pull very tight **(m)**.

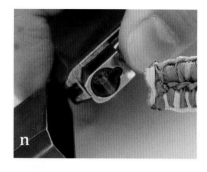

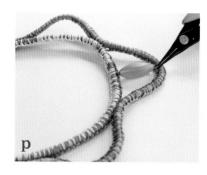

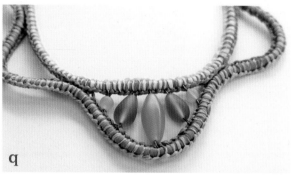

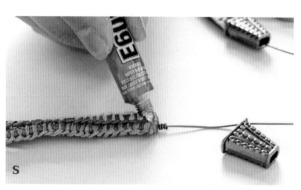

12 Trim the ribbons and paracord. Melt the ribbon and paracord end to hold everything in place **(n)**. Repeat for the other end.

13 String a bead on an eyepin and make a simple loop (Techniques). Repeat with all the beads. Make sure to make the new loop in the same direction as the eyepin's loop so the beads sit correctly on the necklace **(o)**.

14 Attach the large green rice bead in the center of the middle opening. Open an eyepin loop, attach the top middle ribbon loop, and close the loop. Attach the other loop to the bottom **(p)**. Attach the remaining beads, green teardrops, and blue rounds **(q)**. Because the ribbon knots all sit a bit differently and move slightly, it is best to estimate the center and where to attach each bead.

15 Cut two 4-in. pieces of 20-gauge wire. At one end of the necklace slip the wire in between the two paracord pieces under the last teal knot. Bend the wire up into a U shape. Wrap one wire three times around the other. Trim the remaining wrapping wire **(r)**. Repeat on the other side.

16 Apply E6000 jewelry adhesive to each end of the necklace and push an end into a gunmetal cone **(s)**. Make the first half of a wrapped loop with each wire end (Techniques).

17 Cut 6-in. of chain. On one side, slide on the last link of the chain to the loop and complete the wraps. Repeat on the other side with the lobster claw clasp **(t)**.

Acknowledgements

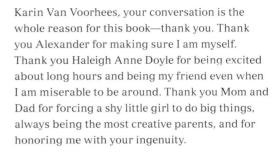

Karin Van Voorhees, your conversation is the whole reason for this book—thank you. Thank you Alexander for making sure I am myself. Thank you Haleigh Anne Doyle for being excited about long hours and being my friend even when I am miserable to be around. Thank you Mom and Dad for forcing a shy little girl to do big things, always being the most creative parents, and for honoring me with your ingenuity.

About the Author

Ashley Kate Bunting

In elementary school she was all about making polymer clay beads. In middle school, she took her first silversmithing class. At the age of 16, Ashley was hired at the local bead shop, where she would work for another 11 years, climbing the ranks to head designer and product developer. At 18, she was off to The University of the Arts to earn a BFA in sculpture. After college Ashley delved deeper into the jewelry world, teaching, starting her own line, designing tutorials, and being published in beading magazines. A few years later, she was discovered by Xuron Corp. and became their jewelry brand ambassador, spreading the love of Maine-made jewelry tools. And now? Well, she's publishing her first book! Ashley hails from Portland, Maine with her mascot Magpie Gem-Hunter (Maggie) the pup and her vintage-dealer fiancé, Alexander.

Knot, Twist, & Weave
Your Way to Beautiful Jewelry!

Melissa Cable shares new methods for altering leather to create textures and patterns in a variety of necklaces, bracelets, cuffs, pendants, and more. Jewelry makers at all skill levels will learn how to work with raw materials and premade pieces to make **20+ upscale leather projects** featuring custom and professional details.

#67036 • $21.99

Introducing a fascinating new technique to bead enthusiasts, fiber artists, and jewelry makers! This thin colorful cord can be wound, bound, and stitched into place with beautiful beads and findings, resulting in fabulous and affordable jewelry. Enjoy **18 unique projects** that combine colorful cording with crystals, seed beads, and more.

#67507 • $21.99

Transform cord and beads into lovely jewelry! Clear, step-by-step instructions and plenty of helpful tips help readers at all skill levels get started with micro macramé, a technique that uses much thinner cords than traditional macramé. Raquel Cruz offers her expertise, tips, and **17 colorful projects**, plus ideas for unique variations.

#67023 • $21.99